little
Christmas
treats

contents

AUSTRALIAN CUP AND
SPOON MEASUREMENTS
ARE METRIC.
A CONVERSION CHART
APPEARS ON PAGE 77.

· ·

Christmas is the time of year when everyone
treats themselves. This book is full of
gorgeous little Christmas delights that will
tempt you to have more than just one.

Pamela Clark

Food Director

Christmas cookies

PASSIONFRUIT CREAM BISCUITS

prep + cook time 1 hour (+ refrigeration & cooling) **makes** 25

125g (4 ounces) butter
2 teaspoons finely grated lemon rind
⅓ cup (75g) caster (superfine) sugar
2 tablespoons golden syrup or treacle
1 cup (150g) self-raising flour
⅔ cup (100g) plain (all-purpose) flour
¼ cup (60ml) passionfruit pulp
passionfruit cream
2 tablespoons passionfruit pulp
90g (3 ounces) butter
1 cup (160g) icing (confectioners') sugar

1 Have butter at room temperature.
2 Beat butter, rind and sugar in small bowl with electric mixer until light and fluffy. Add golden syrup, beat until combined. Stir in sifted dry ingredients and passionfruit pulp.
3 Turn dough onto floured surface, knead gently until smooth. Divide dough in half; roll each portion between sheets of baking paper to 5mm (¼-inch) thickness. Refrigerate 30 minutes.
4 Preheat oven to 180°C/350°F. Line oven trays with baking paper.
5 Cut 25 x 4cm (1½-inch) fluted rounds from each portion of dough; place rounds about 2.5cm (1 inch) apart on trays.
6 Bake biscuits about 10 minutes. Cool on trays.
7 Meanwhile, make passionfruit cream.
8 Spoon passionfruit cream into piping bag fitted with 5mm (¼-inch) fluted tube. Pipe cream onto half the biscuits; top with remaining biscuits. Serve dusted with a little extra sifted icing sugar.
passionfruit cream Strain passionfruit pulp through fine sieve into small jug, discard seeds. Beat butter and sugar in small bowl with electric mixer until light and fluffy. Beat in passionfruit juice.
tip You need about six passionfruit for this recipe.

MACADAMIA AND PECAN SHORTBREAD

prep + cook time 45 minutes **makes** 24

250g (8 ounces) butter
⅓ cup (45g) macadamias
½ cup (60g) pecans
½ cup (110g) caster (superfine) sugar
2 teaspoons vanilla extract
2 cups (300g) plain (all-purpose) flour
½ cup (75g) rice flour
2 tablespoons caster (superfine) sugar, extra

1 Have butter at room temperature.
2 Preheat oven to 160°C/325°F. Lightly grease two oven trays.
3 Finely chop nuts.
4 Beat butter, sugar and extract in small bowl with electric mixer until pale and fluffy. Transfer mixture to large bowl; stir in sifted flours and nuts, in two batches. Press mixture together. Turn dough onto lightly floured surface; knead gently until smooth.
5 Divide dough in half. Roll each portion between sheets of baking paper into 23cm (9-inch) rounds; place on trays. Mark each round into 12 wedges, prick with a fork. Using floured fingers, pinch a frill around each shortbread, sprinkle with extra sugar.
6 Bake shortbread about 20 minutes. Stand on trays 10 minutes before transferring to wire racks to cool.

tips Use a cake pan or plate to mark, then cut the dough into a neat round. Shortbread will keep in an airtight container for up to a month.

STAINED GLASS CHRISTMAS COOKIES

prep + cook time 50 minutes (+ refrigeration) **makes** 32

250g (8 ounces) butter
1 egg
1 vanilla bean
¾ cup (165g) caster (superfine) sugar
1 tablespoon water
2¼ cups (335g) plain (all-purpose) flour
90g (3 ounces) individually wrapped
sugar-free fruit drops, assorted colours

1 Have butter and egg at room temperature.
2 Split vanilla bean lengthways; scrape seeds into medium bowl with butter, egg, sugar and the water. Beat with electric mixer until combined. Stir in sifted flour, in two batches. Knead dough on floured surface until smooth. Cover with plastic wrap; refrigerate 30 minutes.
3 Preheat oven to 180°C/350°F. Line two large oven trays with baking paper.

4 Using a rolling pin, gently tap the wrapped lollies to crush them slightly. Unwrap lollies, separate by colour into small bowls.
5 Roll dough between sheets of baking paper to 5mm (¼-inch) thickness. Cut shapes from dough using 8cm (3¼-inch) long Christmas tree cutter; place cookies on oven trays. Using a 4cm (1½-inch) long Christmas tree or 1.5cm (¾-inch) star cutter, cut out the centre of each tree to make windows. Use a skewer to make a small hole in top of each tree for threading through ribbon, if you like.
6 Bake trees 7 minutes. Remove trays from oven; fill each window with a few same-coloured lolly pieces. Bake a further 5 minutes or until browned lightly. Cool trees on trays.

CINNAMON AND
SOUR CHERRY MACAROONS

prep + cook time 1 hour 15 minutes (+ refrigeration, standing & cooling) **makes** 20

3 egg whites
¼ cup (55g) caster (superfine) sugar
1¼ cups (200g) pure icing
    (confectioners') sugar
1 cup (120g) ground almonds
½ teaspoon ground cinnamon
sour cherry curd
½ cup (100g) drained seeded
    morello sour cherries
3 egg yolks
⅓ cup (75g) caster (superfine) sugar
1 tablespoon lemon juice
2 teaspoons kirsch
60g (2 ounces) unsalted butter
cinnamon sugar
2 tablespoons icing (confectioners') sugar
½ teaspoon ground cinnamon

1 Make sour cherry curd and then cinnamon sugar.
2 Grease oven trays; line with baking paper.
3 Beat egg whites in small bowl with electric mixer until soft peaks form. Add caster sugar, beat until sugar is dissolved. Transfer mixture to large bowl. Fold in sifted icing sugar, ground almonds and cinnamon, in two batches.

4 Spoon mixture into piping bag fitted with 2cm (¾-inch) plain tube. Pipe 4cm (1½-inch) rounds about 2cm (¾-inch) apart on trays. Tap trays on bench so macaroons spread slightly. Dust macaroons with half the sifted cinnamon sugar; stand about 30 minutes or until dry to touch.
5 Meanwhile, preheat oven to 150°C/300°F.
6 Bake macaroons about 20 minutes; cool on trays.
7 Sandwich macaroons with sour cherry curd; dust with remaining sifted cinnamon sugar.
sour cherry curd Blend or process cherries until smooth; you will need 2 tablespoons puree for this recipe. Place egg yolks and sugar in medium heatproof bowl over medium saucepan of simmering water; whisk until thick and sugar is dissolved. Whisk in cherry puree, juice and kirsch. Chop butter; add to bowl, whisk about 5 minutes or until mixture is thick and holds the trail of the whisk. Refrigerate until firm.
cinnamon sugar Sift ingredients into small bowl.
tip Unfilled macaroons will keep in an airtight container for about a week. Filled macaroons will keep in an airtight container in the refrigerator for up to 2 days.

CHOCOLATE WHOOPIE PIES

prep + cook time 35 minutes (+ cooling) **makes** 16

125g (4 ounces) unsalted butter
1 egg
2 teaspoons vanilla extract
½ cup (110g) firmly packed light brown sugar
¾ cup (110g) plain (all-purpose) flour
¼ cup (35g) self-raising flour
1 teaspoon bicarbonate of soda
   (baking soda)
⅓ cup (35g) cocoa powder
⅔ cup (160ml) buttermilk
butter cream filling
60g (2 ounces) unsalted butter
¾ cup (120g) icing (confectioners') sugar
1 tablespoon milk

1 Have butter and egg at room temperature.
2 Preheat oven to 200°C/400°F. Grease and line oven trays with baking paper.
3 Beat butter, extract, sugar and egg in small bowl with electric mixer until light and fluffy.

4 Beat in sifted dry ingredients and buttermilk, in two batches, on low speed, until mixture is smooth.
5 Drop level tablespoons of mixture onto trays, 4cm (1½ inches) apart. Bake about 8 minutes. Cool on trays.
6 Meanwhile, make butter cream filling. Join cooled pies with butter cream filling.
butter cream filling Have butter at room temperature. Beat butter in small bowl with electric mixer until as white as possible. Gradually beat in half the sifted icing sugar and the milk; beat in remaining sifted icing sugar.
tips Whoopie pies are a cross between a soft biscuit and a cake. They are also known as hucklebucks, gobs and BFOs (big fat Oreos). Store filled pies in an airtight container in the refrigerator for up to three days. To make vanilla whoopie pies (also pictured) increase quantity of plain (all-purpose) flour to 1¼ cups (185g), replace brown sugar with caster (superfine) sugar, and omit cocoa powder.

ALMOND BREAD

prep + cook time 1 hour 40 minutes (+ cooling & standing) **makes** 40 slices

3 egg whites
½ cup (110g) caster (superfine) sugar
1 cup (150g) plain (all-purpose) flour
¾ cup (120g) almond kernels

1 Preheat oven to 180°C/350°F. Grease 10cm x 20cm (4-inch x 8-inch) loaf pan.
2 Beat egg whites in small bowl with electric mixer until soft peaks form. Gradually add sugar, beating until dissolved between additions.
3 Fold sifted flour and nuts into egg white mixture; spread mixture into pan. Bake about 30 minutes. Cool bread in pan. Remove bread from pan, wrap in foil; stand overnight.

4 Preheat oven to 150°C/300°F.
5 Using a sharp serrated knife, cut the bread into wafer-thin slices. Place slices, in single layer, on ungreased oven trays. Bake about 45 minutes or until dry and crisp.
tips Almond bread is an excellent accompaniment to desserts such as mousse, sorbet and ice-cream. It will keep for months if stored in an airtight container at room temperature.

PISTACHIO AND ORANGE BLOSSOM MACAROONS

prep + cook time 50 minutes (+ standing & refrigeration) **makes** 16

⅓ cup (45g) unsalted roasted pistachios
3 egg whites
¼ cup (55g) caster (superfine) sugar
green food colouring
1¼ cups (200g) pure icing
   (confectioners') sugar
¾ cup (90g) ground almonds
1 tablespoon pure icing
   (confectioners') sugar, extra
155g (5 ounces) white eating chocolate
¼ cup (60ml) pouring cream
4 teaspoons orange blossom water

1 Grease oven trays; line with baking paper.
2 Process pistachios until ground finely.
3 Beat egg whites in small bowl with electric mixer until soft peaks form. Add caster sugar and a few drops of colouring, beat until sugar dissolves; transfer mixture to large bowl. Fold in ¼ cup of the ground pistachios, sifted icing sugar and ground almonds, in two batches.

4 Spoon mixture into piping bag fitted with 2cm (¾-inch) plain tube. Pipe 4cm (1½-inch) rounds about 2cm (¾ inch) apart onto trays. Tap trays on bench so macaroons spread slightly. Dust macaroons with extra sifted icing sugar; sprinkle with remaining ground pistachios. Stand 30 minutes.
5 Meanwhile, preheat oven to 150°C/300°F.
6 Bake macaroons about 20 minutes. Cool on trays.
7 Chop chocolate finely.
8 Bring cream to the boil in small saucepan, remove from heat; add chocolate, stir until smooth. Stir in orange blossom water. Refrigerate until spreadable.
9 Sandwich macaroons together with chocolate filling.
tips Unfilled macaroons will keep in an airtight container for about a week. Fill macaroons just before serving.

MINI FLORENTINES

prep + cook time 30 minutes (+ standing) **makes** 25

¾ cup (60g) flaked almonds
½ cup (100g) red glacé cherries
¾ cup (120g) sultanas
2 cups (80g) corn flakes
⅔ cup (160ml) sweetened condensed milk
60g (2 ounces) white eating chocolate
60g (2 ounces) dark eating
   (semi-sweet) chocolate

1 Preheat oven to 180°C/350°F. Line oven trays with baking paper.
2 Place nuts on oven tray; roast about 5 minutes or until browned lightly.
3 Quarter cherries. Combine cherries, sultanas, corn flakes, nuts and condensed milk in medium bowl.
4 Drop tablespoons of mixture about 5cm (2 inches) apart on trays. Bake about 5 minutes; cool on trays.
5 Chop white chocolate coarsely. Melt chocolate in small heatproof bowl set over small saucepan of simmering water. Repeat with dark chocolate. Spread the bases of half the florentines with white chocolate; spread remaining florentine bases with dark chocolate. Run fork through chocolate to make waves; stand at room temperature until set.
tip Store florentines in an airtight container in the refrigerator for up to a week.

APPLE, CRANBERRY AND WHITE CHOCOLATE BISCOTTI

prep + cook time 1 hour 25 minutes (+ cooling) **makes** 60

90g (3 ounces) white eating chocolate
1 cup (220g) caster (superfine) sugar
2 eggs
1⅓ cups (200g) plain (all-purpose) flour
⅓ cup (50g) self-raising flour
½ cup (35g) finely chopped dried apple
½ cup (65g) coarsely chopped
    dried cranberries

1 Preheat oven to 180°C/350°F. Grease oven tray.
2 Coarsely grate chocolate.
3 Whisk sugar and eggs in medium bowl until combined; stir in sifted flours then apple, cranberries and grated chocolate.
4 Knead dough on floured surface until smooth. Divide dough in half, roll each portion into a 30cm (12-inch) log; place logs on tray. Bake about 30 minutes. Cool on tray 10 minutes.
5 Reduce oven temperature to 150°C/300°F.
6 Using serrated knife, cut logs diagonally into 5mm (¼-inch) slices. Place slices, in single layer, on ungreased oven trays. Bake biscotti about 30 minutes or until dry and crisp, turning halfway through baking. Cool on wire racks.

tip Biscotti will keep in an airtight container for at least a month.

CHOCOLATE CHUNK AND RASPBERRY COOKIES

prep + cook time 35 minutes **makes** 24

125g (4 ounces) butter
1 egg
90g (3 ounces) dark eating
  (semi-sweet) chocolate
¾ cup (165g) firmly packed light brown sugar
1 teaspoon vanilla extract
1 cup (150g) plain (all-purpose) flour
¼ cup (35g) self-raising flour
⅓ cup (35g) cocoa powder
½ teaspoon bicarbonate of soda
  (baking soda)
125g (4 ounces) frozen raspberries

1 Have butter and egg at room temperature.
2 Preheat oven to 180°C/350°F. Line oven trays with baking paper.
3 Chop chocolate coarsely.
4 Beat butter, sugar, egg and extract in small bowl with electric mixer until combined. Stir in sifted flours, cocoa and soda, in two batches, then stir in chocolate and raspberries.
5 Drop tablespoons of mixture about 5cm (2 inches) apart onto trays; flatten slightly. Bake cookies about 12 minutes. Stand cookies on trays 5 minutes before transferring to a wire rack to cool.
tips Mix and match different coloured chocolates with different berries if you like. Store cookies in an airtight container in the refrigerator for up to a week.

WHITE CHOCOLATE AND CRANBERRY SHORTBREADS

prep + cook time 45 minutes **makes** 26

250g (8 ounces) butter
90g (3 ounces) white eating chocolate
¼ cup (55g) caster (superfine) sugar
1 teaspoon vanilla extract
1½ cups (225g) plain (all-purpose) flour
¼ cup (35g) finely chopped dried cranberries
90g (3 ounces) white chocolate Melts
pink food colouring

1 Have butter at room temperature.
2 Preheat oven to 180°C/350°F. Line oven trays with baking paper.
3 Coarsely grate white eating chocolate.
4 Beat butter, sugar and extract in small bowl with electric mixer until smooth. Transfer to large bowl; stir in sifted flour in two batches, then stir in cranberries and grated chocolate.
5 Drop tablespoons of mixture about 5cm (2 inches) apart onto trays. Bake about 15 minutes; cool on trays.
6 Melt white chocolate Melts in small heatproof bowl over small saucepan of simmering water; tint pink with food colouring. Drizzle chocolate over biscuits; stand at room temperature until set.

Christmas cakes & slices

CHOCOLATE FIG PANFORTE

prep + cook time 1 hour 10 minutes (+ standing) **serves** 20

1 cup (160g) blanched almonds
1 cup (140g) hazelnuts
1 cup (120g) pecans
¾ cup (110g) plain (all-purpose) flour
2 tablespoons cocoa powder
2 teaspoons ground cinnamon
1¾ cups (330g) coarsely chopped
    dried figs
¼ cup (40g) finely chopped glacé orange
100g (3 ounces) dark eating
    (semi-sweet) chocolate
⅓ cup (115g) honey
⅓ cup (75g) caster (superfine) sugar
⅓ cup (75g) firmly packed light brown sugar
2 tablespoons water

1 Preheat oven to 150°C/300°F. Grease deep 20cm (8-inch) round cake pan; line base with baking paper.
2 Place nuts on oven tray; roast 8 minutes or until browned lightly and fragrant.
3 Sift flour, cocoa and cinnamon into large bowl; stir in fruit and nuts.
4 Chop chocolate coarsely. Melt chocolate in small heatproof bowl set over small saucepan of simmering water.
5 Combine honey, sugars and the water in small saucepan; stir over low heat until sugar dissolves. Simmer, uncovered, without stirring, 5 minutes. Pour hot syrup then chocolate into nut mixture; mix well.
6 Press mixture firmly into pan; press a 20cm (8-inch) round of baking paper on top.
7 Bake 40 minutes; cool in pan. Remove panforte from pan, discard baking paper; wrap in foil. Stand overnight before cutting into thin wedges to serve.

BABY CHOCOLATE CHRISTMAS CAKES

prep + cook time 3 hours 20 minutes (+ standing & cooling) **makes** 8

1½ cups (250g) seeded prunes
½ cup (100g) red glacé cherries
2⅓ cups (375g) sultanas
2⅓ cups (375g) coarsely chopped raisins
1½ cups (250g) dried currants
⅓ cup (55g) mixed peel
2 cups (500ml) tokay or port
2 cups (440g) firmly packed dark
    brown sugar
250g (8 ounces) butter
6 eggs
¾ cup (90g) pecans
2 cups (300g) plain (all-purpose) flour
¾ cup (110g) self-raising flour
½ cup (50g) cocoa powder
250g (8 ounces) ready-made white icing

1 Coarsely chop prunes; quarter cherries. Combine all fruit, peel and 1½ cups of the tokay and ½ cup of the brown sugar in large bowl. Cover; stand overnight or for several days.
2 Have butter and eggs at room temperature.
3 Preheat oven to 150°C/300°F. Line bases and sides of eight deep 10cm (4-inch) square cake pans with one layer each of brown paper and baking paper, extending paper 2cm (¾ inch) over sides.

4 Chop nuts coarsely. Beat butter and remaining sugar in large bowl with electric mixer until combined. Beat in eggs, one at a time. Stir butter mixture into fruit mixture. Stir in nuts and sifted dry ingredients, in two batches. Divide mixture into pans; smooth tops.
5 Bake cakes about 1¾ hours. Brush hot cakes with remaining tokay. Cover cakes, in pans, tightly with foil; turn cakes upside down to cool overnight.
6 To decorate, roll icing between sheets of baking paper to 3mm (⅛-inch) thick; cut into 1cm (½-inch) thick ribbons, attach to cake tops with a little water. Using 3cm (1¼-inch) star cutters, cut stars from icing. Brush back of stars with a little water; attach to top of ribbons. Stand for several hours or until dry. Wrap sides of cakes with Christmas ribbon.
tips Tokay is a sweet fortified wine. This recipe will also make one deep 20cm (8-inch) square or one deep 23cm (9-inch) round cake. Line pan with one layer of brown paper and two layers of baking paper. Bake about 3 hours. To store un-iced cakes, turn cakes out of pan, remove lining paper from cakes. Wrap tightly in plastic wrap. Place cakes in an airtight container to protect them. Store in the refrigerator for up to 3 months, or freeze for up to a year. Thaw frozen cakes in the refrigerator for 2 days.

LITTLE CHRISTMAS CAKES

prep + cook time 1 hour 15 minutes (+ standing & cooling) **makes** 20

1 cup (150g) raisins
1 cup (140g) seeded dates
1 cup (200g) dried figs
¼ cup (50g) red glacé cherries
½ cup (125g) chopped glacé fruit
    (such as pineapple, apricot, peach)
2 cups (320g) sultanas
1 cup (160g) dried currants
¾ cup (180ml) brandy
250g (8 ounces) butter
4 eggs
1 cup (220g) firmly packed dark brown sugar
¼ cup (85g) orange marmalade
1¾ cups (260g) plain (all-purpose) flour
½ cup (75g) self-raising flour
1½ teaspoons ground cinnamon
1 teaspoon mixed spice
red glacé cherries, to decorate
lemon icing
3 cups (480g) pure icing
    (confectioners') sugar
1 tablespoon lemon juice
¼ cup (60ml) water, approximately

1 Coarsely chop raisins, dates, figs and cherries.
2 Combine all fruit in large bowl; stir in ½ cup of the brandy. Cover; stand in a cool, dark place overnight or for up to one week, stirring every day.
3 Have butter and eggs at room temperature.
4 Preheat oven to 160°C/325°F. Lightly grease 20 holes of two 12-hole (⅓-cup/80ml) muffin pans. Line bases with baking paper.
5 Beat butter, sugar and marmalade in small bowl with electric mixer until combined. Beat in eggs, one at a time. Transfer mixture to large bowl; stir in sifted dry ingredients, in two batches. Stir in fruit mixture.
6 Divide mixture between pan holes; smooth tops. Bake about 30 minutes. Brush hot cake tops with remaining brandy.
7 Stand cakes in pans 5 minutes before turning, top-side up, onto wire rack to cool.
8 Meanwhile, make lemon icing.
9 Working quickly, spoon a heaped tablespoon of warm icing over each cake. Press a cherry in centre of each cake; stand cakes until icing sets.
lemon icing Sift icing sugar into medium heatproof bowl. Add juice and enough of the water to make a thick paste. Stir over medium saucepan of simmering water until warm and of a pouring consistency.
tip If icing thickens, place over simmering water until a pouring consistency.

DRIED APPLE
AND CRANBERRY MUESLI SLICE

prep + cook time 45 minutes (+ cooling) **makes** 24

2 cups (220g) untoasted natural muesli
1 cup (150g) self-raising flour
½ cup (30g) coarsely chopped dried apples
½ cup (65g) dried cranberries
½ cup (110g) caster (superfine) sugar
155g (5 ounces) butter
¼ cup (90g) honey
2 eggs
pink icing
½ cup (80g) icing (confectioners') sugar
1 tablespoon hot water
¼ teaspoon vegetable oil
pink food colouring

1 Preheat oven to 180°C/350°F. Grease 20cm x 30cm (8-inch x 12-inch) rectangular pan; line base and long sides with baking paper, extending paper 5cm (2 inches) over sides.
2 Combine muesli, sifted flour, fruit and sugar in large bowl.
3 Chop butter coarsely.
4 Combine butter and honey in small saucepan; stir over low heat until smooth. Whisk eggs in small bowl with fork until combined. Stir butter mixture and eggs into muesli mixture until combined. Spread mixture into pan; bake about 25 minutes. Cool slice in pan.
5 Meanwhile, make icing. Drizzle icing over slice before cutting.
pink icing Combine sifted icing sugar, the water and oil in small bowl; tint icing pink.
tip Store slice in an airtight container for up to a week.

WHITE CHOCOLATE, PINEAPPLE AND COCONUT SLICE

prep + cook time 1 hour (+ cooling & standing) **makes** 35

90g (3 ounces) butter
250g (8 ounces) white eating chocolate
440g (14 ounces) canned crushed pineapple
   in natural juice
½ cup (110g) caster (superfine) sugar
2 eggs
1½ cups (225g) plain (all-purpose) flour
½ cup (75g) self-raising flour
½ cup (40g) desiccated coconut
1½ cups (240g) pure icing
   (confectioners') sugar
⅓ cup (25g) shredded coconut

1 Preheat oven to 160°C/325°F. Grease 24cm x 32cm (9½-inch x 13-inch) swiss roll pan; line base and long sides with baking paper, extending paper 5cm (2 inches) over sides.
2 Chop butter and chocolate coarsely. Stir butter and chocolate in medium saucepan over low heat until smooth. Cool 10 minutes.

3 Meanwhile, drain pineapple well over medium bowl. Reserve 2 tablespoons juice.
4 Stir caster sugar, eggs, sifted flours, desiccated coconut and drained pineapple into chocolate mixture; spread mixture into pan. Bake about 35 minutes. Cool slice in pan before icing.
5 Meanwhile, sift icing sugar into medium heatproof bowl; stir in reserved pineapple juice. Set bowl over medium saucepan of simmering water; stir until icing is spreadable.
6 Spread icing over slice; sprinkle with shredded coconut. Stand at room temperature until icing sets before cutting.
tips Do not overheat or over-stir chocolate mixture or it will "split". Store slice in an airtight container for up to a week.

BEST-EVER FUDGE BROWNIES

prep + cook time 1 hour **makes** 96

185g (6 ounces) unsalted butter
300g (10 ounces) dark eating
　(semi-sweet) chocolate
¼ cup (25g) cocoa powder
1 cup (220g) firmly packed light
　brown sugar
¾ cup (165g) caster (superfine) sugar
2 teaspoons vanilla extract
4 eggs
1½ cups (225g) plain (all-purpose) flour
2 teaspoons cocoa powder, extra

1 Preheat oven to 170°C/340°F. Grease
20cm x 30cm (8-inch x 12-inch) rectangular
pan; line base and long sides with baking
paper, extending paper 5cm (2 inches)
over sides.
2 Chop butter and chocolate coarsely.

3 Stir butter and chocolate in medium
saucepan over low heat until smooth.
Remove from heat; whisk in sifted cocoa,
sugars and extract until smooth. Cool
5 minutes.
4 Stir eggs and sifted flour into
chocolate mixture. Pour mixture into pan;
spread evenly.
5 Bake about 40 minutes. Cool
brownie in pan. Dust with extra sifted
cocoa before cutting.
tips The mixture should be barely warm
when the eggs and flour are added. Use a
bamboo skewer to test if the brownie is
cooked. The skewer should feel moist if you
want a fudgy brownie; if not, bake the
brownie another 5 minutes or so. Store
brownies in an airtight container in the fridge
for up to a week. They are best served at
room temperature.

FRANGIPANE CHERRY SQUARES

prep + cook time 45 minutes **makes** 24

170g (5½ ounces) butter
3 eggs
¾ cup (165g) caster (superfine) sugar
1 cup (120g) ground almonds
⅓ cup (50g) plain (all-purpose) flour
300g (10 ounces) frozen cherries
¼ cup (20g) flaked almonds
2 teaspoons icing (confectioners') sugar

1 Have butter and eggs at room temperature.
2 Preheat oven to 180°C/350°F. Grease 20cm x 30cm (8-inch x 12-inch) rectangular pan; line base and long sides with baking paper, extending paper 5cm (2 inches) over sides.
3 Beat butter and sugar in medium bowl with electric mixer until light and fluffy; beat in eggs until combined. Stir in ground almonds and sifted flour; spread mixture into pan. Top with cherries, pressing down gently; sprinkle with flaked almonds. Bake about 30 minutes. Cool slice in pan.
4 Dust slice with sifted icing sugar before cutting. Serve warm or at room temperature.
tip Store squares in an airtight container for up to 4 days.

SPICY MIXED FRUIT SLICE

prep + cook time 1 hour 10 minutes (+ refrigeration) **makes** 16

250g (8 ounces) cold butter
2 cups (300g) plain (all-purpose) flour
⅓ cup (55g) icing (confectioners') sugar
2 teaspoons mixed spice
1 tablespoon caster (superfine) sugar
fruit filling
1 cup (140g) coarsely chopped seeded
   dried dates
1 cup (190g) coarsely chopped dried figs
½ cup (80g) currants

1 Preheat oven to 180°C/350°F. Grease 20cm x 30cm (8-inch x 12-inch) rectangular pan; line base and long sides with baking paper, extending paper 5cm (2 inches) over sides.
2 Chop butter. Process flour, icing sugar, butter and spice until ingredients combine. Press half the dough into pan. Bake 15 minutes, cool. Cover and refrigerate remaining dough.
3 Meanwhile, make fruit filling.
4 Using wet hand, press filling over base. Roll remaining dough between sheets of baking paper until large enough to cover filling; trim to fit. Brush dough with a little water; sprinkle with caster sugar.
5 Bake slice about 35 minutes. Cool slice in pan before cutting.
fruit filling Blend or process fruit until chopped finely.
tips Use a palette knife to press dough evenly over base of pan. Store slice in an airtight container for up to a week.

CHOCOLATE DRAMBUIE FRUIT CAKES

prep + cook time 4 hours 30 minutes (+ standing & cooling) **serves** 36

2¼ cups (335g) raisins
1½ cups (250g) seeded prunes
1½ cups (210g) seeded dried dates
⅔ cup (140g) red glacé cherries
2⅓ cups (375g) sultanas
1⅔ cups (270g) dried currants
¾ cup (125g) mixed peel
1⅓ cups (330ml) drambuie
⅓ cup (120g) honey
1 tablespoon finely grated lemon rind
250g (8 ounces) butter
6 eggs
1½ cups (330g) firmly packed dark
    brown sugar
90g (3 ounces) dark eating
    (semi-sweet) chocolate
1¼ cups (150g) pecans
2 cups (300g) plain (all-purpose) flour
1 cup (150g) self-raising flour
¼ cup (25g) cocoa powder
whole pecans and glacé cherries, extra

1 Coarsely chop raisins, prunes and dates; quarter cherries. Combine fruit, peel, 1 cup of the liqueur, honey and rind in large bowl. Cover; store in a cool, dark place overnight or for up to one week, stirring every day.
2 Have butter and eggs at room temperature.

3 Preheat oven to 120°C/250°F. Grease 6-hole (¾-cup/180ml) texas muffin pan. Grease deep 22cm (9-inch) round or deep 19cm (8-inch) square cake pan; line base and side(s) with four thicknesses of baking paper, extending paper 5cm (2 inches) above side(s).
4 Beat butter and sugar in medium bowl with electric mixer until combined. Beat in eggs, one at a time. Stir butter mixture into fruit mixture.
5 Grate chocolate coarsely; chop nuts coarsely. Stir chocolate, nuts and sifted dry ingredients into fruit mixture, in two batches.
6 Fill each muffin pan hole, level to the top, with mixture; spread remaining mixture into cake pan. Decorate tops with extra pecans and glacé cherries, if you like.
7 Bake muffins about 1½ hours (cake can stand while muffins are baking). Brush hot muffins with some of the remaining liqueur; cover with foil, cool in pan.
8 Increase oven temperature to 150°C/300°F. Bake large cake about 3 hours; brush hot cake with remaining liqueur. Cover hot cake with foil; cool in pan overnight.
tips Drambuie is a whisky-based liqueur. Cakes can be made up to three months ahead; store in an airtight container in the refrigerator or freeze for up to 12 months. If you don't want to make the mini cakes, spread cake mixture into a deep 25cm (10-inch) round or deep 22cm (9-inch) square cake pan; bake about 4 to 4½ hours.

LAMINGTONS

prep + cook time 1 hour 10 minutes **makes** 16

6 eggs
⅔ cup (150g) caster (superfine) sugar
⅓ cup (50g) cornflour (cornstarch)
½ cup (75g) plain (all-purpose) flour
⅓ cup (50g) self-raising flour
2 cups (160g) desiccated coconut
chocolate icing
15g (½ ounce) butter
4 cups (640g) icing (confectioners') sugar
½ cup (50g) cocoa powder
1 cup (250ml) milk

1 Have eggs at room temperature.
2 Preheat oven to 180°C/350°F. Grease 20cm x 30cm (8-inch x 12-inch) rectangular pan; line base and long sides with baking paper, extending paper 5cm (2 inches) over sides.
3 Beat eggs in large bowl with electric mixer about 10 minutes or until thick and creamy; gradually add sugar, beating until dissolved between additions. Triple-sift flours; fold into egg mixture.
4 Spread mixture into pan; bake about 35 minutes. Turn cake immediately onto baking paper-covered wire rack to cool.
5 Meanwhile, make chocolate icing.
6 Cut cake into 16 pieces. Place coconut into medium bowl. Dip each piece of cake in icing; drain off excess. Toss squares in coconut. Place lamingtons on wire rack to set.
chocolate icing Melt butter in small saucepan. Sift icing sugar and cocoa in medium heatproof bowl; stir in butter and milk. Set bowl over medium saucepan of simmering water; stir until icing is of a coating consistency.

HONEY NUT SQUARES

prep + cook time 50 minutes (+ cooling & refrigeration) **makes** 35

125g (4 ounces) unsalted butter
½ cup (110g) caster (superfine) sugar
1 egg yolk
1 cup (150g) plain (all-purpose) flour
⅓ cup (50g) self-raising flour
⅔ cup (230g) honey
⅓ cup (75g) firmly packed light brown sugar
90g (3 ounces) unsalted butter, extra
2 tablespoons thickened (heavy) cream
1 cup (120g) pecans
½ cup (80g) almond kernels
½ cup (70g) roasted hazelnuts

1 Have butter at room temperature.
2 Preheat oven to 160°C/325°F. Grease 20cm x 30cm (8-inch x 12-inch) rectangular pan; line base and long sides with baking paper, extending paper 5cm (2 inches) over sides.
3 Beat butter, caster sugar and egg yolk in small bowl with electric mixer until light and fluffy. Stir in sifted flours. Press mixture evenly over base of pan. Bake 15 minutes.
4 Stir honey, brown sugar and extra butter in medium saucepan over low heat until sugar is dissolved. Bring to the boil; boil, uncovered, without stirring, 2 minutes. Add cream; boil, stirring, 1 minute. Remove from heat. Stir in nuts until coated in caramel mixture. Working quickly, pour nut mixture over base; spread evenly with spatula.
5 Bake about 15 minutes. Cool slice in pan. Refrigerate 2 hours before cutting.

tip Store squares in an airtight container for up to 4 days.

APRICOT SQUARES

prep + cook time 30 minutes **makes** 30

1⅔ cups (250g) dried apricots
500g (1 pound) plain sweet biscuits
250g (8 ounces) butter
¾ cup (165g) firmly packed light brown sugar
395g (12½ ounces) canned sweetened
   condensed milk
⅓ cup (25g) desiccated coconut

1 Grease 23cm x 32cm (9-inch x 13-inch) swiss roll pan; line base and long sides with baking paper, extending paper 5cm (2 inches) over sides.
2 Process apricots until finely chopped; transfer to large bowl. Process biscuits, in two batches, until finely crushed; transfer to bowl with apricots.
3 Chop butter coarsely. Combine butter, sugar and condensed milk in medium saucepan; whisk over low heat until butter is melted. Bring to the boil, whisking constantly. Remove from heat; stir into apricot mixture.
4 Spread mixture into pan; smooth surface. Sprinkle with coconut; cool. Refrigerate until firm before cutting into squares or bars.
tip Depending on size of the food processor, the apricots can be processed in two batches.

Christmas confectionery

SALTED CARAMEL TRUFFLES

prep + cook time 40 minutes (+ refrigeration & freezing) **makes** 25

⅓ cup (75g) caster (superfine) sugar
2 tablespoons water
⅔ cup (160ml) pouring cream
200g (6½ ounces) dark eating
   (semi-sweet) chocolate
1 teaspoon sea salt flakes
200g (6½ ounces) milk eating chocolate

1 Combine sugar and the water in small saucepan; stir over heat, without boiling, until sugar dissolves. Bring to the boil; boil, uncovered, without stirring, until golden brown. Add cream; stir over low heat until toffee pieces melt.
2 Meanwhile, chop dark chocolate finely. Remove toffee mixture from heat; stir in chocolate and half the salt until smooth. Refrigerate mixture overnight.
3 Working with a quarter of the chocolate mixture at a time (keep remainder refrigerated), roll rounded teaspoons of mixture into balls; place on foil-lined tray. Freeze until firm.
4 Chop milk chocolate. Place chocolate in small heatproof bowl over small saucepan of simmering water; stir until smooth. Working quickly, using two forks, dip truffles in milk chocolate. Return truffles to tray; sprinkle with remaining salt. Refrigerate truffles until firm.

SEA SALT AND CASHEW CARAMELS

prep + cook time 30 minutes (+ cooling) **makes** 40

1½ cups (330g) caster (superfine) sugar
1½ cups (375ml) thickened (heavy) cream
¼ cup (90g) glucose syrup
1½ cups (225g) unsalted roasted cashews
2 teaspoons sea salt

1 Grease an 18cm x 28cm (7¼-inch x 11¼-inch) slice pan. Line base and sides with baking paper, extending paper 5cm (2 inches) over sides.
2 Stir sugar, cream and glucose in medium saucepan until sugar is dissolved. Bring to the boil; boil, uncovered, until mixture reaches 120°C (248°F) on a candy thermometer.
3 Add nuts and sprinkle with half the salt, do not stir. Pour caramel into pan; sprinkle with remaining salt. Cool.
4 Use a warm oiled sharp knife to cut caramel into pieces.
tips Glucose syrup is also called liquid glucose; it's available in most supermarkets and delicatessens. Store caramels between layers of baking paper in an airtight container in a cool dry place for up to a week. When packaging as a gift, layer between sheets of baking paper.

PISTACHIO WHITE CHOCOLATE BRITTLE

prep + cook time 25 minutes (+ standing) **serves** 16

1 cup (140g) unsalted, roasted,
   shelled pistachios
2 cups (440g) caster (superfine) sugar
½ cup (125ml) water
2 tablespoons rosewater
1 tablespoon dried rose petals
90g (3 ounces) white eating chocolate

1 Line oven tray with baking paper.

2 Chop nuts coarsely.

3 Stir sugar and the water in medium saucepan over heat, without boiling, until sugar dissolves. Stir in rosewater; bring to the boil. Boil, uncovered, without stirring, until golden brown. Allow bubbles to subside; add nuts. Pour mixture onto tray; sprinkle with rose petals. Leave to set at room temperature.

4 Chop chocolate. Place chocolate in small heatproof bowl over small saucepan of simmering water; stir until smooth. Turn brittle over. Spread chocolate over flat side of brittle. Leave to set at room temperature. Break brittle into pieces.

tip Dried rose petals are available from specialist food stores.

DARK CHOCOLATE AND NOUGAT FUDGE BARS

prep + cook time 15 minutes (+ refrigeration) **makes** 42

360g (11½ ounces) dark eating
  (semi-sweet) chocolate
395g (12½ ounces) canned sweetened
  condensed milk
30g (1 ounce) butter
200g (6½ ounces) soft nougat,
  chopped coarsely

1 Grease 20cm x 30cm (8-inch x 12-inch) rectangular pan; line base and long sides with baking paper, extending paper 5cm (2 inches) over sides.
2 Chop chocolate coarsely. Combine chocolate, condensed milk and butter in large saucepan; stir over low heat until smooth. Remove from heat; stir in nougat. Pour mixture into pan, smooth surface with a wet spatula. Refrigerate about 3 hours or until firm before cutting.
tip Store bars in an airtight container in the refrigerator for up to a week, or freeze for up to four weeks.

MARSHMALLOW TREATS

prep + cook time 30 minutes (+ refrigeration) **makes** 55

200g (6½ ounces) butter
395g (12½ ounces) canned sweetened
    condensed milk
1 cup (220g) firmly packed light brown sugar
¼ cup (25g) cocoa powder
2 teaspoons vanilla extract
3¾ cups (375g) plain sweet biscuit crumbs
300g (9½ ounces) pink and
    white marshmallows
1½ cups (120g) desiccated coconut

1 Combine chopped butter, condensed milk, sugar, sifted cocoa and extract in medium saucepan; stir over low heat until smooth. Remove from heat; stir in biscuit crumbs.
2 Using damp hands, roll three heaped teaspoons of mixture around each marshmallow, pressing firmly to enclose marshmallows. Place coconut in small shallow bowl; roll balls in coconut, place on trays. Refrigerate until firm.

FIG AND NUT LOGS

prep + cook time 45 minutes (+ standing) **makes** 2 logs (each log makes 20 pieces)

150g (4½ ounces) dark eating
  (semi-sweet) chocolate
1 cup (190g) coarsely chopped dried figs
¾ cup (100g) dried cherries
1 teaspoon finely grated orange rind
¼ cup (60ml) brandy
⅔ cup (90g) coarsely chopped roasted
  unsalted pistachios
⅔ cup (70g) coarsely chopped
  roasted walnuts
⅓ cup (60g) finely chopped
  candied clementines
¼ cup (45g) finely chopped glacé ginger
½ teaspoon ground cinnamon
¼ teaspoon mixed spice
2 sheets 15cm x 23cm (6-inch x 9½-inch)
  confectioners' rice paper

1 Chop half the chocolate finely. Chop remaining chocolate coarsely.
2 Melt coarsely chopped chocolate in small heatproof bowl over small saucepan of simmering water.
3 Process figs, cherries, rind and half the brandy until fruit is chopped finely. Transfer mixture to large bowl; stir in nuts, clementines, ginger, spices and finely chopped and melted chocolate.
4 Spoon mixture down long side of each rice paper sheet. Roll each sheet to enclose filling and make a log shape. Pinch along top of each log to make a triangle shape; brush rice paper with remaining brandy.
5 Wrap logs in baking paper; stand overnight at room temperature. Serve logs sliced thickly.
tip Candied clementines are available from specialty food stores and delicatessens; if you can't find them, use glacé oranges.

WHITE CHRISTMAS SLICE

prep time 20 minutes (+ refrigeration) **makes** 32

500g (1 pound) white eating chocolate
1 cup (35g) rice bubbles
1 cup (160g) sultanas
1 cup (80g) desiccated coconut
⅔ cup (110g) finely chopped dried apricots
½ cup (100g) halved red glacé cherries

1 Grease 20cm x 30cm (8-inch x 12-inch) rectangular pan; line base and long sides with baking paper, extending paper 5cm (2 inches) over sides.
2 Chop chocolate coarsely. Melt chocolate in large heatproof bowl over large saucepan of simmering water. Remove from heat; quickly stir in remaining ingredients.
3 Press mixture firmly into pan. Refrigerate 2 hours or until firm before cutting.

CHERRY SQUARES
WITH COCONUT ICE FROSTING

prep + cook time 35 minutes (+ refrigeration) **makes** 35

125g (4 ounces) butter
¼ cup (55g) caster (superfine) sugar
⅓ cup (80ml) light corn syrup
8 cups (320g) corn flakes
½ cup (40g) toasted shredded coconut
1 cup (100g) halved red glacé cherries
coconut ice frosting
1½ cups (240g) pure icing
   (confectioners') sugar
1 cup (80g) desiccated coconut
1 egg white
2 tablespoons boiling water, approximately
pink food colouring

1 Grease 20cm x 30cm (8-inch x 12-inch) rectangular pan; line base and long sides with baking paper, extending paper 5cm (2 inches) over sides.
2 Chop butter coarsely. Stir butter, sugar and syrup in small saucepan over low heat until sugar dissolves; bring to the boil. Reduce heat; simmer, uncovered, without stirring, 5 minutes.
3 Meanwhile, coarsely crush corn flakes with hands in large bowl until approximately half the volume; stir in coconut and cherries.
4 Stir butter mixture into cornflake mixture. Spread mixture into pan; press down firmly. Cover; refrigerate 30 minutes or until firm.
5 Make coconut ice frosting.
6 Spread frosting over slice; cut into squares when firm.
coconut ice frosting Sift icing sugar into medium bowl; stir in coconut and egg white until combined. Add enough of the water until icing is spreadable; tint frosting pink.
tip Store squares in an airtight container in the refrigerator for up to a week.

CHOC-MALT SLICE

prep + cook time 20 minutes (+ refrigeration) **makes** 40

250g (8 ounces) plain chocolate biscuits
280g (9 ounces) choc-coated malt balls
100g (3 ounces) unsalted butter
½ cup (125ml) sweetened condensed milk
400g (12½ ounces) milk eating chocolate
1 tablespoon vegetable oil

1 Grease 20cm x 30cm (8-inch x 12-inch) rectangular pan; line base and long sides with baking paper, extending paper 5cm (2 inches) over sides.
2 Process 200g (6½ ounces) of the biscuits until fine; chop remaining biscuits coarsely.
3 Reserve 40 whole choc-malt balls; coarsely chop 1 cup of the remaining balls. Reserve any extra choc-malt balls for another use.

4 Chop butter. Stir butter and condensed milk in small saucepan over low heat until smooth.
5 Combine processed and chopped biscuits with chopped choc-malt balls in medium bowl; stir in butter mixture. Press mixture into pan. Refrigerate 30 minutes.
6 Chop chocolate coarsely. Stir chocolate and oil in medium heatproof bowl over medium saucepan of simmering water until smooth; spread over biscuit base. Top with reserved choc-malt balls. Refrigerate about 1 hour or until set before cutting.
tips Use un-iced, unfilled plain biscuits for this recipe. Store slice in an airtight container in the refrigerator for up to 4 days.

CHOC-ORANGE FUDGE

prep + cook time 55 minutes (+ refrigeration, cooling & standing) **makes** 60

575g (1¼ pounds) dark eating
  (semi-sweet) chocolate
2 teaspoons finely grated orange rind
3 cups (660g) caster (superfine) sugar
1 cup (220g) firmly packed light brown sugar
⅓ cup (115g) glucose syrup
1 cup (250ml) pouring cream
½ cup (125ml) milk
90g (3 ounces) butter
45g (1½ ounces) white eating chocolate
orange food colouring

1 Grease 20cm x 30cm (8-inch x 12-inch) rectangular pan; line base and long sides with baking paper, extending paper 5cm (2 inches) over sides.
2 Chop chocolate coarsely.
3 Place 185g (6 ounces) of the dark chocolate in small heatproof bowl over small saucepan of simmering water; stir until smooth. Stir in half the rind. Spread chocolate over base of pan; refrigerate until set.
4 Meanwhile, stir sugars, syrup, cream, milk and another 200g (6½ ounces) of the dark chocolate in medium saucepan over heat, without boiling, until sugar dissolves. Bring to the boil; boil, without stirring, about 10 minutes or until mixture reaches 116°C/235°F on a candy thermometer. Remove from heat, leaving thermometer in mixture.

5 Chop butter, add to chocolate mixture; do not stir.
6 Cool fudge up to 1½ hours or until the temperature of the mixture drops to 40°C/80°F. Remove thermometer. Stir fudge with wooden spoon about 10 minutes or until a small amount dropped from the spoon holds its shape. Spread fudge over chocolate in pan; smooth surface. Cover with foil; stand at room temperature about 2 hours or until set.
7 Place remaining dark chocolate in small heatproof bowl over small saucepan of simmering water; stir until smooth. Stir in remaining rind. Repeat to melt white chocolate; tint orange. Working quickly, spread dark chocolate over slice; drizzle with orange chocolate. Pull a skewer through chocolate mixture for a feather and fan effect. Stand at room temperature until chocolate sets before cutting.
tips Using a candy thermometer will ensure perfect results. Glucose syrup is also called liquid glucose; it's available in most supermarkets and delicatessens. Store fudge in an airtight container for up to a week. Slice is best served at room temperature.

COCONUT TRUFFLES

prep + cook time 40 minutes (+ refrigeration) **makes** 30

360g (11½ ounces) white eating chocolate
½ cup (125ml) coconut cream
2 teaspoons finely grated lime rind
2 teaspoons finely grated lemon rind
1¼ cups (95g) shredded coconut

1 Chop chocolate coarsely.

2 Combine chocolate, coconut cream and rind in small saucepan; stir over low heat until smooth. Transfer mixture to small bowl, cover; refrigerate 3 hours or overnight, until firm.

3 Working with a quarter of the chocolate mixture at a time (keep remainder refrigerated), roll rounded teaspoons of mixture into balls; place on foil-lined tray. Refrigerate truffles until firm.

4 Working quickly, roll truffles in coconut, return to tray; refrigerate until firm.

SUGAR AND SPICE ALMONDS

prep + cook time 30 minutes (+ cooling) **makes** 5 cups

1½ cups (240g) pure icing
   (confectioners') sugar
1½ tablespoons ground cinnamon
5 cups (800g) almond kernels

1 Preheat oven to 180°C/350°F. Line large baking dish with baking paper.

2 Sift icing sugar and cinnamon together twice into medium bowl.

3 Place nuts in colander; rinse under cold water. Tip wet nuts into baking dish. Sift the cinnamon mixture over nuts; toss to coat.

4 Roast almonds about 20 minutes, stirring halfway through cooking, or until fragrant and browned. Cool in dish; they will become crisp on cooling.

5 Separate almonds and store in airtight jars or package in cellophane bags.

tip Nuts will keep in an airtight container or in sealed bags in a cool, dry spot for up to one month.

ALMONDS flat, pointy-tipped nuts with a pitted brown shell enclosing a creamy white kernel which is covered by a brown skin.

blanched brown skins removed.

flaked paper-thin slices.

meal also called ground almonds.

slivered small pieces cut lengthways.

BAKING PAPER also known as parchment paper or baking parchment – is a silicone-coated paper that is primarily used for lining baking pans and oven trays so cakes and biscuits won't stick, making removal easy.

BAKING POWDER a raising agent consisting mainly of two parts cream of tartar to one part bicarbonate of soda.

BICARBONATE OF SODA (BAKING SODA) an acid and alkaline combination, which when moistened and heated, gives off carbon dioxide that aerates and lightens the mixture during baking.

BISCUITS also known as cookies.

butternut snap crunchy cookie made with golden syrup, oats and coconut.

gingernuts a plain biscuit made with golden syrup and ginger.

shortbread plain buttery biscuit with a crumbly texture.

BUTTER we use salted butter unless stated otherwise; 125g is equal to 1 stick (4 ounces).

CASHEWS plump, kidney-shaped, golden-brown nuts with a distinctive sweet, buttery flavour and containing about 48 per cent fat. Because of this high fat content, they should be kept, sealed tightly, under refrigeration to avoid becoming rancid.

CHOCOLATE

choc bits also known as chocolate chips or chocolate morsels; available in milk, white and dark chocolate. They hold their shape in baking and are ideal for decorating.

dark eating also known as semi-sweet or luxury chocolate; made of a high percentage of cocoa liquor and cocoa butter, and little added sugar. Unless stated otherwise, we use dark eating chocolate in this book as it's ideal for use in desserts and cakes.

Melts small discs of compound milk, white or dark chocolate ideal for melting and moulding.

milk most popular eating chocolate, mild and very sweet; similar in make-up to dark with the difference being the addition of milk solids.

white contains no cocoa solids but derives its sweet flavour from cocoa butter. Very sensitive to heat.

CINNAMON available both in the piece (called sticks or quills) and ground into powder; one of the world's most common spices, used universally as a sweet, fragrant flavouring for both sweet and savoury foods.

CINNAMON SUGAR a combination of ground cinnamon and caster sugar. It is available from supermarkets in the spice section.

COCO POPS chocolate-flavoured puffed rice breakfast cereal.

COCOA POWDER also known as unsweetened cocoa; cocoa beans (cacao seeds) that have been fermented, roasted, shelled, ground into powder then cleared of most of the fat content.

COCONUT

desiccated concentrated, dried, unsweetened, finely shredded coconut.

shredded unsweetened thin strips of dried coconut flesh.

CONFECTIONERS' RICE PAPER is made from a dough made from the pith of an Asian shrub called the rice-paper plant (or rice-paper tree), not from rice. It resembles a grainy sheet of paper and is used in confectionery and baking. It can be bought from specialty food stores; don't confuse it with the rice paper used in recipes such as Asian rice paper rolls, which needs soaking to soften.

CORN FLAKES breakfast cereal made of dehydrated then baked crisp flakes of corn.

CORN SYRUP, LIGHT an imported product available in some supermarkets, delicatessens and health food stores. Made from cornstarch, it is a popular ingredient in American cooking for frostings, jams and jellies.

CORNFLOUR also known as cornstarch. Available made from corn or wheat (wheaten cornflour gives a lighter texture in cakes); used as a thickening agent in cooking.

CRANBERRIES fruit available dried and frozen; have a rich, astringent flavour and can be used in cooking sweet and savoury dishes. The dried version can usually be substituted for or with other dried fruit.

CREAM we used fresh cream, also known as pure or pouring cream unless otherwise stated. It contains no additives and has a minimum fat content of 35 per cent.

sour a thick commercially cultured soured cream with a minimum fat content of 35 per cent.

thick (double) a dolloping cream with a minimum fat content of 45 per cent.

thickened (heavy) a whipping cream containing thickener. Minimum fat content of 35 per cent.

CREAM CHEESE commonly called philadelphia or philly; a soft cow's milk cheese, its fat content ranges from 14 to 33 per cent.

CREME FRAICHE a mature, naturally fermented cream (minimum fat content 35 per cent) with a velvety texture and slightly tangy, nutty flavour. This French variation of sour cream can boil without curdling and be used in sweet and savoury dishes.

CURRANTS, DRIED tiny, almost black raisins so-named after a grape that originated in Corinth, Greece.

CUSTARD POWDER instant powdered mixture used to make pouring custard; similar to North American instant pudding mixes.

EGGS we use large chicken eggs weighing an average of 60g unless stated otherwise in the recipes in this book. If a recipe calls for raw or barely cooked eggs, exercise caution if there is a salmonella problem in your area, particularly in food eaten by children and pregnant women.

EXTRACT/ESSENCE an essence is either a distilled concentration of a food quality or an artificial creation of it. An extract is made by extracting the flavour from a food product. Essences and extracts keep indefinitely if stored in a cool dark place.

FLOUR

plain also known as all-purpose; unbleached wheat flour is the best for baking: the gluten content ensures a strong dough and a light result.

potato is made from cooked potatoes that have been dried and ground into a fine flour.

rice a very fine flour, made from ground rice.

self-raising all-purpose plain or wholemeal flour with baking powder and salt added; make yourself with plain or wholemeal flour sifted with baking powder in the proportion of 1 cup flour to 2 teaspoons baking powder.

FRUIT MINCE also known as mincemeat. A mixture of dried fruits such as raisins, sultanas and candied peel, nuts, spices, apple, brandy or rum. Is used as a filling for cakes, puddings and fruit mince pies.

GELATINE we use dried (powdered) gelatine in this book; it's also available in sheet form known as leaf gelatine. A thickening agent made from either collagen, a protein found in animal connective tissue and bones, or certain algae (agar-agar). Three teaspoons of dried gelatine (8g or one sachet) is about the same as four gelatine leaves. The two types are interchangable but leaf gelatine gives a much clearer mixture than dried gelatine; it's perfect in dishes where appearance matters.

GLACE CHERRIES or candied cherries; boiled in heavy sugar syrup then dried.

GLACE GINGER fresh ginger root preserved in sugar syrup.

GLUCOSE SYRUP also known as liquid glucose, made from wheat starch; used in jam and confectionery and available at health food stores and supermarkets.

GOLDEN SYRUP a by-product of refined sugarcane; pure maple syrup or honey can be substituted. Treacle is more viscous, and has a stronger flavour and aroma than golden syrup (which has been refined further and contains fewer impurities, so is lighter in colour and more fluid).

GROUND GINGER also called powdered ginger; used as a flavouring in baking but cannot be substituted for fresh ginger.

HAZELNUTS also known as filberts; plump, grape-sized, rich, sweet nut having a brown skin that is removed by rubbing heated nuts together vigorously in a tea-towel. Hazelnut meal is made by grounding the hazelnuts to a coarse flour texture for use in baking or as a thickening agent.

HONEY the variety sold in a squeezable container is not suitable for the recipes in this book.

JAM also known as preserve or conserve; most often made from fruit.

LOLLIES a confectionery also known as sweets or candy.

MACADAMIAS native to Australia; fairly large, slightly soft, buttery rich nut. Used to make oil and macadamia butter; equally good in salads or cakes and pastries; delicious eaten on their own. Should always be stored in the fridge to prevent their high oil content turning them rancid.

MARMALADE a preserve, usually based on citrus fruit.

MARSALA a fortified Italian wine produced in the region surrounding the Sicilian city of Marsala.

MARSHMALLOWS pink and white; made from sugar, glucose, gelatine and cornflour.

MILK we use full-cream homogenised milk unless otherwise specified.

evaporated unsweetened canned milk from which water has been extracted by evaporation. Evaporated skim or low-fat milk has 0.3 per cent fat content.

full-cream powder instant powdered milk made from whole cow milk with liquid removed and emulsifiers added.

sweetened condensed a canned milk product consisting of milk with more than half the water content removed and sugar added to the remaining milk.

MIXED DRIED FRUIT a combination of sultanas, raisins, currants, mixed peel and cherries.

MIXED SPICE a classic spice mixture generally containing caraway, allspice, coriander, cumin, nutmeg and ginger, although cinnamon and other spices can be added. It is used with fruit and in cakes.

MUESLI also known as granola, a combination of grains (mainly oats), nuts and dried fruits. Some manufacturers toast their product in oil and honey, adding crispness and kilojoules.

NOUGAT a popular confection in southern Europe; made from sugar or honey, roasted nuts, sometimes candied fruits and beaten egg white (for soft nougat) or caramelised sugar (for hard nougat).

NUTMEG a strong, pungent spice ground from the dried nut of an evergreen tree native to Indonesia. Usually found ground but the flavour is more intense from a whole nut, available from spice shops, so it's best to grate your own.

PEANUT BUTTER peanuts ground to a paste; available in crunchy and smooth varieties.

PEANUTS also known as groundnut, not in fact a nut but the pod of a legume. We mainly use raw (unroasted) or unsalted roasted peanuts.

PECANS native to the US and now grown locally; pecans are golden brown, buttery and rich. Walnuts are a good substitute.

PISTACHIOS green, delicately flavoured nuts inside hard off-white shells. Available salted or unsalted in their shells; you can also buy shelled.

POLENTA also known as cornmeal; a flour-like cereal made of dried corn (maize). Also the dish made from it.

RAISINS dried sweet grapes (traditionally muscatel grapes).

RHUBARB a plant with long, green-red stalks; becomes edible when cooked.

RICE BUBBLES a small puffed rice breakfast cereal.

ROLLED OATS flattened oat grain rolled into flakes and traditionally used for porridge. Instant oats are also available, but we prefer to use traditional oats for baking.

SHERRY fortified wine consumed as an aperitif or used in cooking. Sold as fino (light, dry), amontillado (medium sweet, dark) and oloroso (full-bodied, very dark).

STAR ANISE a dried star-shaped pod with seeds with an astringent aniseed flavour; commonly used to flavour stocks and marinades.

SUGAR we use coarse, granulated table sugar, also known as crystal sugar, unless otherwise specified.

brown a soft, finely granulated sugar retaining molasses for its characteristic colour and flavour.

caster also known as superfine or finely granulated table sugar.

demerara small-grained golden-coloured crystal sugar.

icing also known as confectioners' sugar or powdered sugar; pulverised granulated sugar crushed together with a small amount of cornflour.

pure icing also called confectioners' sugar or powdered sugar.

raw natural brown granulated sugar.

SULTANAS dried sweet grapes of the sultana variety.

VANILLA BEAN dried, long, thin pod from a tropical golden orchid; the minuscule black seeds inside the bean are used to impart a luscious vanilla flavour in baking and desserts. Place a whole bean in a jar of sugar to make the vanilla sugar often called for in recipes; a bean can be used three or four times.

extract obtained from vanilla beans infused in water; a non-alcoholic version of essence.

WALNUTS as well as being a good source of fibre and healthy oils, nuts contain a range of vitamins, minerals and other beneficial plant components called phytochemicals. Walnuts contain the beneficial omega-3 fatty acids.

WEET-BIX also known as ruskets; wholewheat malted breakfast biscuit.

CONVERSION CHART

MEASURES

One Australian metric measuring cup holds approximately 250ml, one Australian metric tablespoon holds 20ml, one Australian metric teaspoon holds 5ml.

The difference between one country's measuring cups and another's is within a 2- or 3-teaspoon variance, and will not affect your cooking results. North America, New Zealand and the United Kingdom use a 15ml tablespoon. All cup and spoon measurements are level. The most accurate way of measuring dry ingredients is to weigh them. When measuring liquids, use a clear glass or plastic jug with metric markings.

We use large eggs with an average weight of 60g.

DRY MEASURES

METRIC	IMPERIAL
15g	½oz
30g	1oz
60g	2oz
90g	3oz
125g	4oz (¼lb)
155g	5oz
185g	6oz
220g	7oz
250g	8oz (½lb)
280g	9oz
315g	10oz
345g	11oz
375g	12oz (¾lb)
410g	13oz
440g	14oz
470g	15oz
500g	16oz (1lb)
750g	24oz (1½lb)
1kg	32oz (2lb)

LIQUID MEASURES

METRIC	IMPERIAL
30ml	1 fluid oz
60ml	2 fluid oz
100ml	3 fluid oz
125ml	4 fluid oz
150ml	5 fluid oz
190ml	6 fluid oz
250ml	8 fluid oz
300ml	10 fluid oz
500ml	16 fluid oz
600ml	20 fluid oz
1000ml (1 litre)	1¾ pints

LENGTH MEASURES

METRIC	IMPERIAL
3mm	⅛in
6mm	¼in
1cm	½in
2cm	¾in
2.5cm	1in
5cm	2in
6cm	2½in
8cm	3in
10cm	4in
13cm	5in
15cm	6in
18cm	7in
20cm	8in
23cm	9in
25cm	10in
28cm	11in
30cm	12in (1ft)

OVEN TEMPERATURES

These oven temperatures are only a guide for conventional ovens.
For fan-forced ovens, check the manufacturer's manual.

	°C (CELSIUS)	°F (FAHRENHEIT)
Very slow	120	250
Slow	150	275-300
Moderately slow	160	325
Moderate	180	350-375
Moderately hot	200	400
Hot	220	425-450
Very hot	240	475

The imperial measurements used in these recipes are approximate only. Measurements for cake pans are approximate only. Using same-shaped cake pans of a similar size should not affect the outcome of your baking. We measure the inside top of the cake pan to determine sizes.

INDEX

Published in 2012 by ACP Books, Sydney

ACP Books are published by ACP Magazines Limited,
a division of Nine Entertainment Co.

54 Park St, Sydney
GPO Box 4088, Sydney, NSW 2001.

phone (+61)2 9282 8618; fax (+61)2 9126 3702

acpbooks@acpmagazines.com.au; www.acpbooks.com.au

ACP BOOKS

Publishing Director, ACP Magazines · Gerry Reynolds

Publisher · Sally Wright

Editorial & Food director · Pamela Clark

Creative Director · Hieu Chi Nguyen

Published and Distributed in the United Kingdom by Octopus Publishing Group

Endeavour House

189 Shaftesbury Avenue

London WC2H 8JY

United Kingdom

phone (+44)(0)207 632 5400; fax (+44)(0)207 632 5405

info@octopus-publishing.co.uk;

www.octopusbooks.co.uk

Printed by Toppan Printing Co., China

International Foreign Language Rights · Brian Cearnes, ACP Books bcearnes@acpmagazines.com.au

A catalogue record for this book is available from the British Library.
ISBN 9781742453330